Affirmations
& Crystals

CLAIRE TITMUS

Affirmations & Crystals

365 Crystals, Messages and Affirmations to Empower You Every Day

quadrille

THIS BOOK BELONGS TO

_____

INTRODUCTION

This book has been written with love, light and positivity to uplift your day and to empower and ignite your most brilliant future. Think of it as a spiritual go-to for your daily wellbeing, your own motivational speaker.

However you deal with the tests of life, *words* have a profound effect. They can shape your beliefs, affect your emotional reactions, heal you or break you, and now it's time to use them to YOUR advantage.

Gain the confidence to take charge of your existence, feel supported by your invisible higher forces, and awaken your intuition to gain answers that you may be in a quandary over, as guided by the crystals in this book.

It's important to know that the affirmations and messages in this book need feeding with your intention. You could, of course, read them just once, but each time you repeat them out loud or in your mind, you'll strengthen them and plant them into your subconscious. The words will gain momentum and you will help them grow in power, in turn giving you the strength, inspiration, motivation or support that you need.

HOW TO GET THE MOST
OUT OF THE BOOK

There are no rules. You are invited to use this book however you wish. However, my favourite ways are:

◊   Read it conventionally from page 1 on the day you bought it, taking inspiration from a page a day for the next year. Then, dip in and out when you need it.

◊   Ask the book for specific guidance. Hold the book in your hands or place one hand on the book. Close your eyes and ask your question out loud or silently in your mind's eye. Turn or flick through the pages: the message or affirmation you land on is your guidance.

◊   If you want more from any affirmation, repeat it with absolute belief that it is true two to three times a day for at least two weeks to awaken the power of the words. Doing this will be positively life-changing.

◊ Use the book to gain wisdom as to which crystal fits best with different messages and affirmations, and in turn different areas of your day-to-day life. Remember, crystal knowledge is power. The crystals that accompany the daily entries have been chosen specifically to support you further. You do not need a large piece; a smaller tumbled stone or piece of jewellery will be ideal.

Please note: So as not to overwhelm you with lists of crystals, I have shared just one per message or affirmation. However, if you feel inspired to choose a different crystal from your collection, lean into your intuition and go with it. Crystals have a mystical habit of choosing you when you need them the most. Intuition is a very powerful energy, as it is often in tune with our destiny and life path.

#1

You deserve every ounce of happiness in your life, and there is even more around the corner. Don't try too hard to look for it. New happiness will flood into your life when you least expect it.

Orange Calcite welcomes joy and sunshine, and lifts your spirits.

#2

I will follow my own dreams.

Moonstone has a powerful energy that will give you clarity and foresight as you head down your chosen path.

#3

I am the master of my wealth. I am open to receiving money in abundance.

Citrine attracts money and asks fortunate opportunities to cross your path.

#4

I will not let the pain of my past stop me from moving on. I choose to let go of what no longer serves me.

Rhodonite helps you to move on from past emotional love trauma and let go with ease.

#5

Inspiration sparks our motivation on the quest to be our best self and is delivered in many ways. What may be inspiring for someone else may not necessarily be inspiring for you, and that's absolutely fine. We may all find that spark in different things. If a certain path doesn't feel right, be honest with those pushing you and carve your own path. Happiness knows no bounds, and you hold the key to it.

Citrine helps you become the master of your destiny and attract what you need.

#6

Only I truly know the answer. I will listen to my gut instinct and intuition.

Labradorite connects you to your intuition. Work with labradorite during a deep breathing exercise or meditation to connect to your third eye. The answers you are looking for will become clearer.

#7

I will succeed at what I put my mind to.

Red Jasper helps you harness inner strength
and self-motivation.

#8

Divine timing can't be rushed. The Universe has grand plans for you, full of success, love, luck and joy. While you can welcome your own dreams and set intentions, there is also a deep-rooted plan for you. Just be patient and your true destiny will not pass you by. Exciting days are ahead. Trust the process.

Clear Quartz feeds your intentions and existing energy with a spark of clarity, raising your vibrations to work alongside the Universe.

#9

I will achieve my goals with confidence
and success.

Lapis lazuli is a warrior stone that will give you
the confidence and focus to go after exactly
what you want.

#10

I will use the inspiration I feel right now to put
my plans into action.

Garnet keeps passion and motivation burning deep
within. Carry or wear garnet to keep that fire lit.

#11

I am lucky in all that I do. Luck flows to me easily.

Pyrite lifts your spirits and confidence like
sunshine, and attracts success and fortune.

#12

There are always planetary alignments affecting the energy around us. Just know that you can access this at any time. Today, harness the wisdom of loved ones passed. Ask for guidance for any problem or question you may have, and ask for the answer to be delivered in clarity. You may feel alone but there is so much support around you spiritually and cosmically. The Universe and angels have your back and will deliver.

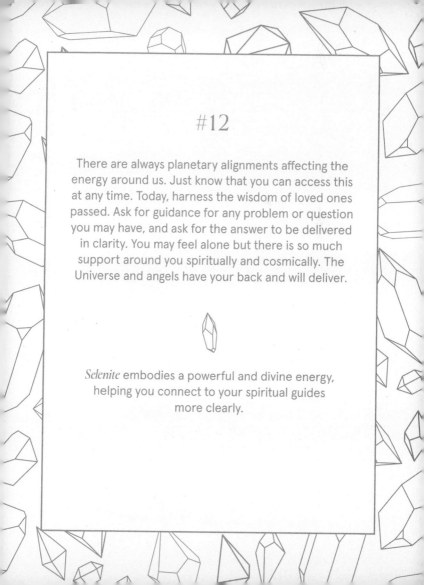

Selenite embodies a powerful and divine energy, helping you connect to your spiritual guides more clearly.

#13

I am at peace and I give myself permission to heal
with each deep breath.

Amethyst promotes peace, tranquillity and calm. It
is also great for soothing headaches and healing
inflammation and sore muscles.

#14

I open my eyes to recognize the unexpected
opportunities coming my way.

Citrine attracts new financially abundant opportunities,
whether it's a way to save, earn or receive money.

#15

I am more capable than I could ever imagine.

Amethyst calms your mind and nerves while you focus on the task in hand.

#16

The energy at play is strong and could bring a wave of long forgotten memories to help propel you towards a brighter future. There is a call for balance, and to set realistic goals and strategies. Revisit lessons learned, or remind yourself of good moments that you can intertwine in your day today. You are on the right path and exciting opportunities are for the taking.

Fluorite helps awaken your inner focus, while blocking any negativity from clouding your judgement.

#17

It's my time to show exactly who I am, each and every fabulous part.

Amazonite helps you love yourself for all that you are with poise, calm and self-acceptance.

#18

I believe in my abilities.

Carnelian gives an extra dose of empowerment. Keep carnelian close by to strengthen your determination and inner confidence.

#19

I see money flowing into my bank. I am a money magnet.

Citrine attracts endless abundance and money-making opportunities.

#20

You may feel a little out of sorts today, as you are encouraged to let go of what no longer serves you in life. It is difficult to move on or let things go, but it is important to make way for bigger and brighter things. Reflect on the good in your life and give thanks for all that you are grateful for. Your spiritual cheerleaders and angels have your back more than ever, and give you the confidence to make the right decision.

Aquamarine symbolizes the calming waters of the sea. It is wonderful for clarity, cleansing and closure. It also helps you bring unfinished business to a conclusion.

#21

Every second I get closer to being bathed in light.

Tiger's eye and its gold hues are like rays of sun,
bringing you inner sunshine.

#22

I am calm. I can think clearly. I am focused.

Amethyst helps calm your mind and focus on
what is causing the issue.

#23

I give myself permission to relax and take time for me.

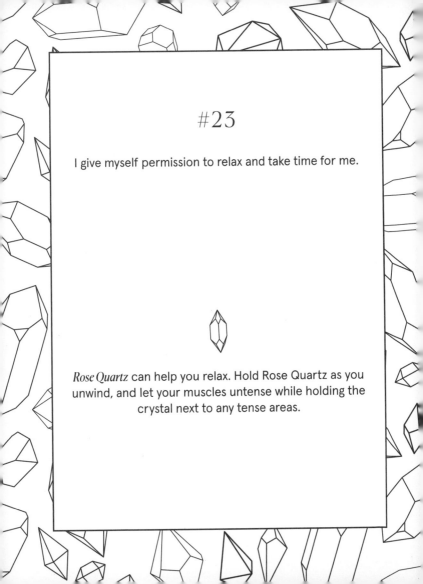

Rose Quartz can help you relax. Hold Rose Quartz as you unwind, and let your muscles untense while holding the crystal next to any tense areas.

#24

I am intelligent and focused. I will achieve greater things. I am going to make myself so proud.

Fluorite gives you mental clarity while banishing negative distractions.

#25

Actions speak louder than words, with persistence being the key to success. Don't let any setbacks stop you from moving forwards; they're just a test to see how much you really want what you are working towards. See them as valuable lesson on your road to greatness and success. There is usually more than one way forwards. Trust in yourself to take the right path.

Labradorite is a wonderful crystal for transformation, and helps you persevere with the task in hand.

#26

My dream job or opportunity is on its way to me.

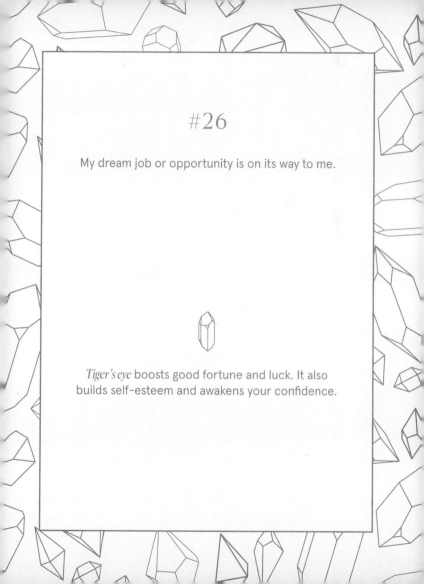

Tiger's eye boosts good fortune and luck. It also
builds self-esteem and awakens your confidence.

#27

I am always in the right place at the right time.
I am a luck magnet and I attract miracles.

Jade increases luck and good fortune and lets
it flow to you.

#28

Today is a new adventure, a blank page and a new opportunity to say what you want to say.

Amethyst can be worn for courage and clarity when facing the day and embracing your new adventures.

#29

I let go of the feelings of anger. I acknowledge my anger but refuse to act on it.

White Howlite helps calm to be your number one emotion as you work through a situation.

#30

Know that good times lie ahead of you. If your instinct is telling you that you really need to get out of a situation or change course, trust yourself. These feelings tend to mean that you are the one that will have to make the choice or the first move. Often, the door must close behind you before the door in front of you can fully open. Believe in your strength.

Sodalite gives you the clarity to delve into your own psyche and unlock hidden feelings.

#31

Be proud of every fibre of your being and look at how
you have faced your challenges so far. You have fought
many silent battles, but faced them all head on with
sheer grit and determination. You are inspiring.

Bloodstone brings you courage and resilience as you
face the realities of your life's path and face any
difficulties. It gives you inner strength.

#32

I choose to be kind and caring to myself.

Rose Quartz can be carried to remind yourself
that love starts within, and to surround yourself
in a gentle energy.

#33

I value the energy each relationship brings to my life and I will take the steps to build the bridges with those that mean everything to me. Love is stronger than any disagreement.

Smokey Quartz blocks any negativity and grounds your emotions as you make the next move to resolve your situation.

#34

Communicate your feelings. Whether it's written down
or spoken out loud, it is important for your wellbeing
to get it all out and lighten your load.

Sodalite is fantastic for helping you speak your truth
with confidence and determination while keeping
your cool.

#35

I am determined to be the best version of myself.

Carnelian can be used to strengthen your motivation
and drive in whatever task you've set yourself.

#36

I attract fortune and success into my life. All the resources I need to succeed are within me, and I know I am capable.

Sunstone can be kept close at work for success in all areas of your life.

#37

It's important to look after your wellbeing and mental and physical health. This will allow you to function at your best, so it's important to lavish yourself with ample amounts of self-care, even if it's just ten minutes a day. It's not selfish to give yourself quality time to feel your best.

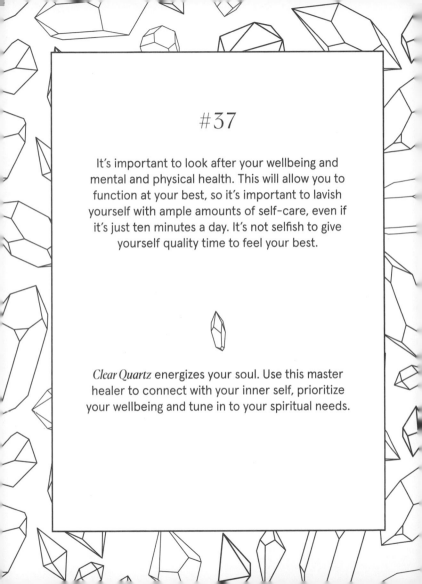

Clear Quartz energizes your soul. Use this master healer to connect with your inner self, prioritize your wellbeing and tune in to your spiritual needs.

#38

Focus on your blessings today. Don't allow stress
to take away all that you are grateful for right now.
Focus on the good around you to lift you higher.

Amethyst is your personal calming angel. Hold it close
to allow its energy to soothe you and bring back
clarity to how much good you have in life, and to
put everything into perspective.

#39

Embrace the day and look around at all the positives in your life. No matter how hard things may seem, they are there. Appreciate all that you have; show gratitude and you'll attract more of the same. You hold the key to your happiness.

Tiger's eye awakens a deep joy and happiness within your soul. Think of it as your personal fortune maker as it attracts golden opportunities into your life.

#40

True love begins at home, with myself.

Red Jasper will help you awaken your self-esteem, blocking any negative thoughts that may well be preventing you from appreciating yourself for the glorious person you are.

#41

I am worthy of joy and happiness. It's my time to experience this in abundance.

Orange Calcite will awaken a deep inner joy.

#42

I will embrace all the opportunities and situations today brings.

Black Obsidian grounds any heightened emotions and protects your energy from unwanted outside influences as you face all tasks with success.

#43

Positive energies are surrounding and guiding you. All will go according to plan when you have total confidence in your abilities. Get creative and be creative. View your life as a blank canvas and set the wheels in motion.

Black Tourmaline helps positivity flood to you easily. Work with this powerful crystal to block and cleanse the negativity around you.

#44

I am allowed to be happy, successful and content.
I am my own priority.

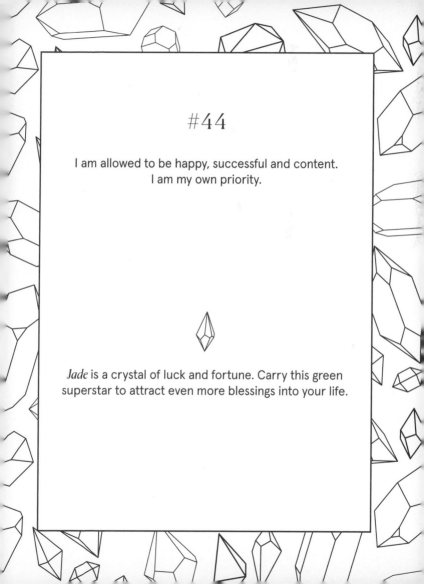

Jade is a crystal of luck and fortune. Carry this green superstar to attract even more blessings into your life.

#45

Love will win through all of the obstacles.

Rose Quartz nurtures your self-love from within and attracts healthy relationships.

#46

I think wisely before reacting to any situation I am upset about.

White Howlite is your spiritual calming friend that will help you make sense of the emotions you are feeling.

#47

If I can visualize it, I can do it. Nothing will stop me.

Aura Quartz connects you to your angels and helps you see your self-worth.

#48

I have all the energy I need to accomplish my goals. I
nourish my body with all that it needs.

Kyanite will make the impossible seem possible and the
most difficult projects doable.

#49

Everything is going to work out for the greater good.
You may be a little uncertain, but be assured that the
Universe has an amazing plan for you. Your wishes,
goals and intentions have been heard. Now you just
need to believe you deserve to receive. Visualize right
now you living your desires. What does it feel like? Let
that motivate you.

Manifestation Quartz can be used to achieve your goals.
Make a wish upon this crystal and allow its energy to
work with your angels to manifest it into existence.

#50

Time you enjoy wasting is not wasting time. Don't feel guilty for going with the flow.

Amethyst soothes your energy and calms frayed nerves.

#51

Showing your true self isn't something to be feared, it is something to be embraced. Let your beautiful soul and personality radiate as and when YOU want to. Those who love you will truly love you for your real authentic self. Go shine!

Snowflake Obsidian helps you see the true value in yourself and the amazing person you are.

#52

I ask for what I want and am prepared to receive it.

Pyrite attracts luck, success and abundance. Wear or carry this super sparkly crystal to reap the reward.

#53

I am confident in my abilities to communicate
my needs and desires.

Sodalite helps you speak your truth with clarity
and ease.

#54

Everything is going to work out for your greater good. Bright times are ahead. You may be a little uncertain if this is really for you, but be assured that the Universe has an amazing plan for you. In fact, we are excited for you: your manifestations and intentions have been heard. Now you just need to believe you deserve the very best.

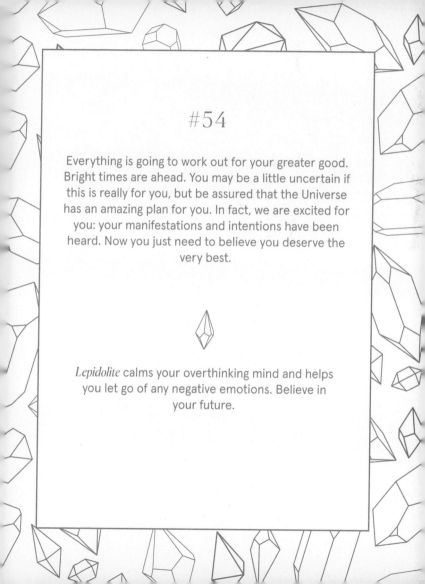

Lepidolite calms your overthinking mind and helps you let go of any negative emotions. Believe in your future.

#55

I have the power to attract wealth and fortune into my life. Abundance is all around me and in everything I do.

Citrine welcomes success in all areas of your life. Whatever you put your mind to will be a winner.

#56

I embrace change with confidence.

Labradorite guides you through transition
and change with confidence.

#57

I am my own best friend. I am a beautiful person. Real love starts with me.

Rose Quartz invites your heart chakra to be open to appreciating your incredible self.

#58

Take back your power. Something or someone from your past seems to be holding you back. It's time to take strength and believe in your confidence to face and overcome any challenges. You deserve to feel free, and there's a brighter day ahead of you when you do.

Angelite helps you build a connection with your angels and communicate better throughout the angelic realm, especially during meditation.

#59

Look at things from a different perspective,
and see the things change.

Blue Calcite helps you see situations with more
clarity and calmness as you take back control
of your emotions.

#60

Luck is flowing into my life abundantly. Good fortune
is with me today and always.

Jade builds lucky energy. Make a wish on it to really
ignite its support.

#61

It is okay to feel however I feel. Tomorrow is a fresh start.

Fluorite keeps negativity and stress at bay as you process your thoughts. Think of it as a shield deflecting others' feelings and emotions, and soothing yours.

#62

I am valuable and make a difference in my job. I trust my career journey.

Garnet keeps you grounded and focused on the task in hand.

#63

Be prepared for truths to make themselves known. You've been strong for far too long, but finally someone will feel the need to speak out and free a weight off your shoulders. Remember, you may have been through some tough times, but the page is turning and your strength will see you through.

Clear Quartz helps clear the fog in your mind and encourages you to think clearly.

#64

I am constantly evolving into a better person. I free myself from self-destructive doubt.

Pink Tourmaline helps you heal from past experiences and traumas and supports you to grow and evolve.

#65

Despite current upheavals, manifestation is happening on a rapid level. Everything you aspire to is in motion. Keep visualizing and make sure every decision you make helps you on the path to receiving. Life is about to change up a gear.

Citrine attracts abundance. Set your intentions with a piece of citrine in your hand to energize every intention and attract them to you.

#66

I am healthy, vibrant, happy and radiant, and
I deserve to be so.

Red Jasper helps your inner strength shine through with
confidence as you take on new fitness activities.

#67

Work towards letting go of anything that hurts your soul. If it has hurt you, it has already played its part in your life. Ask yourself: what did that situation teach me? What was the lesson I took away from it? Looking at difficult times with this mindset is a game changer. Growth is important, and you can and will rise stronger.

Labradorite can be used to work through any change and transformation with confidence and strength. Use this crystal to see your true potential.

#68

No one is me, and that is my divine power.

Amethyst helps you dig deep and find your
inner strength with guidance from your
spiritual cheerleaders.

#69

Good healthy energy flows to me in abundance.

Mookaite Jasper helps you attract and tap into your inner
strength and wisdom, which is beneficial when making
huge decisions.

#70

It's time to regain power over your life in all areas. You control your destiny. Keep pushing forwards knowing that there's nothing you can't accomplish.

Blue Tiger's eye will inspire you to speak from your own personal power and assert yourself to stand up for what you believe in.

#71

I am worthy of love and happiness. I attract healthy
love and friendship to me in abundance.

Rhodonite helps you let go of outdated emotions and
feelings that are holding you back. Use this crystal to
grow a deeper love within current relationships, too.

#72

You can go either way. Go with what your inner vibes are telling you.

Malachite will help you gain clarity and analyze your feelings with clarity.

#73

Instead of resisting the current, try going with the flow. Accept that you are where you are right now, but that you won't be there forever. Move forwards with confidence knowing you can achieve anything you set your mind to. Your capabilities are limitless, just trust the process.

Labradorite banishes the fears and insecurities you may be feeling. This crystal will encourage you to have faith in all that you are and trust in the Universe.

#74

I will take time out to just switch off today.

Lithium Quartz helps calm the mind and body, and is perfect for when you want to relax quickly if your me time is short.

#75

It's time to reflect and get ready to put your forwards plans in motion. Now is the time to bring new hopes and dreams to life. Stand strong in your beliefs and persevere on your path. Ask for help where needed and allow the support to happen.

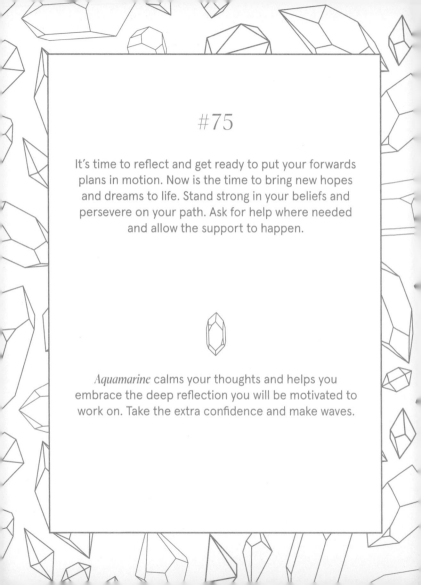

Aquamarine calms your thoughts and helps you embrace the deep reflection you will be motivated to work on. Take the extra confidence and make waves.

#76

A big opportunity is coming your way that you may
not have been expecting. While it may seem very
exciting, just be sure that you're comfortable with all
the minor and big details. It's going to add a new
fun element to your day.

Jade attracts luck and good fortune into your life.

#77

I am attracting great opportunities. I am brave enough to choose what is good for me.

Citrine is great for success in business or in the workplace, as it attracts good opportunities, deals and money.

#78

It's easy to give up when you experience the first failure, but you've got to keep going. Your next attempt could be the successful one. Keep going, show determination, and all will work out. Success is within reach and you deserve it.

Red Tiger's eye welcomes success by igniting motivation, encouraging energy and giving you perseverance when you need it most.

#79

I find inspiration in the most unlikely of places.

Clear Quartz gives instant clarity when on the path to your truths.

#80

Sing, dance and laugh like no one is listening. Today, take a moment to indulge in what you love doing the most. The joy will be an amazing tonic for your soul.

Citrine has a gentle, joyful energy that will lift you up spiritually and mentally as it attracts warmth and happiness into your day.

#81

Take any opportunity you are presented with to better yourself or your life. You have the courage needed to go for it. You are capable of amazing things.

White Howlite keeps your mind calm so you can think clearly when facing and soothing your fears.

#82

Do one thing today that you will applaud yourself for,
and that takes you out of your comfort zone.

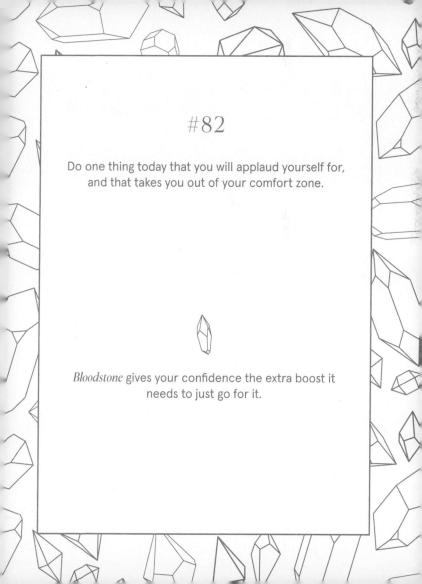

Bloodstone gives your confidence the extra boost it
needs to just go for it.

#83

Overthinking and overwhelm can harm your inner peace. Today, take some time to meditate and ground yourself, and take one day at a time.

Fluorite will help you think with focus and determination. Take back control and stop worry in its tracks by deflecting the negative energies that could be causing it.

#84

The mistakes I made yesterday are the lessons I learnt for today.

Honey Calcite helps you see things more brightly by giving focus to your memories, and allowing your mind to think straight as you look forwards.

#85

My heart is open to receiving and giving love. The love that I seek also seeks me.

Malachite helps you feel stable, safe and secure when beginning to look for a new love or friendships.

#86

I am not my anxieties. They do not define me.
I am safe and in control.

Amethyst calms your mind and soul to give you
confidence as you face what you need to face.

#87

Tune in to your intuition when looking for answers. There is a spiritual solution to every problem you may face. Allow your soul the opportunity to inspire, influence and guide you. It will always show you the way. The key is in you trusting it.

Blue Obsidian connects you to your spirit guides for clarification during dreams, meditation and relaxation.

#88

I believe in myself and my skills. I have the power to change the world.

Fluorite focuses the mind as you use your skills for your greater good.

#89

My positive thoughts and actions renew my health
and body.

Clear Quartz is the master healer. It is great for energy
and works with all ailments. Hold it close to the area in
need. It also pairs up with any other crystal to amplify
its healing energy.

#90

Dreams remain dreams without action, so this is your sign to make a start today! No matter how small the action, it's still a step in the right direction.

Rose Quartz can be carried for loving, supportive energy as you strive forwards.

#91

I am balanced and centred and I allow healing energy to flow freely through my body. My body can do amazing things.

Moonstone will help you feel balanced and restored within your energy field.

#92

I embrace the transformative power of my
spiritual awakening.

Apophyllite helps you to make changes,
empowering you as you navigate new
spiritual situations with confidence.

#93

I hold the key to my own happiness.

Peridot helps you move away from darkness and embrace your own inner light.

#94

Your incredible work and kind actions aren't going unnoticed. Expect to receive back what you put out into your world. An avalanche of good will flow your way. It may appear in an unexpected form, but you deserve it.

Citrine attracts an abundance of good fortune and joy into your life.

#95

Special moments are different for each of us, so hold on to treasured memories and embrace the moments that make you fulfilled. Take photos, make notes, share the joy and be comfortable in who you are. Only you know what makes you smile.

Lapis lazuli helps you keep your memories alive and to reignite deep feelings that you want to relive.

#96

Sometimes, taking the easy path isn't the most fulfilling. Taking a chance on the unexpected can lead to bigger opportunities and more contentment. You've got what it takes.

Red Jasper awakens your inner strength and self-belief.

#97

I trust in the divine plan for my life's journey.

Rainbow Moonstone connects you to your higher being
and purpose with ease as you align with your path.

#98

Self-belief and knowing you're worthy of a bigger and brighter future are key right now. You are deserving of anything you put your mind to. Obstacles aren't road blocks, they're just tests to see how much you really want the end goal.

Botswana Agate helps you see the positives of the ebbs and flows of life, and how they can bring positives to your day.

#99

This is your sign to appreciate yourself for all that you are. Self-acceptance is powerful. Work on finding the contentment in your existence, and love your beautiful soul. You're a force to be reckoned with.

Rose Quartz gives you a warm spiritual hug and a dose of self-love. Carry it close by to empower your day.

#100

I am guided every step by my angels.

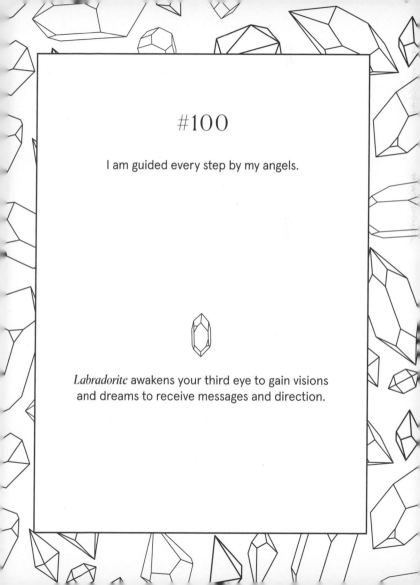

Labradorite awakens your third eye to gain visions
and dreams to receive messages and direction.

#101

It's okay to be different. It's okay to live my truth. It's okay to be everything I want in life.

Sunstone lift your spirits and confidence as you show the world the real you.

#102

You need to ride the storms to find the rainbows.
The darkness will fade to light and you will be
stronger. The sunshine is breaking through.
You've got this.

Smokey Quartz awakens your positive thoughts and
balances your emotions. Protect your energy as
you ride the difficult days, and try not to absorb
the energy of others around you.

#103

You'll always be drawn back to what is truly meant for you. The path will find its way back to guide you to your destiny. If you're unsure about a decision you've made, know that you'll be guided. Go with your intuition.

Clear Quartz helps you gain clarity when your mind feels muddled. Ask for guidance and you'll receive it.

#104

I am a creator and I attract miracles.

Golden healer Quartz ignites your inner goddess
or warrior and calls upon the Universe to
deliver your miracles.

#105

It's okay to say no to situations or decisions that make you feel uncomfortable.

Pyrite gives you confidence and will boost your assertiveness and ability to stand up for what you believe in.

#106

Believe in yourself, your skills, talents and abilities a little bit more. You are more than capable to set the wheels in motion or finish the project on your mind. Start the day as you mean to go on and go for it.

Apatite energizes your focus and will help expand your knowledge so you can strive forwards.

#107

I am a strong, capable person. I am determined and will succeed.

Red Jasper has a positive impact on your intentions and will help you to chase your dreams, giving you strength and confidence.

#108

I have achieved things in the past, and I can and will achieve them again.

Lapiz lazuli awakens your self-awareness. Channel the experience and wisdom from past adventures.

#109

My personal boundaries are important and I am allowed to protect them.

Black Tourmaline can be carried or placed at your front door to deflect bad wishes, bad intentions and negative energies. If any pass through your door or aura they'll be absorbed and transmuted.

#110

When you're feeling confused and need clarity it is
important to remember that what is truly is meant for
you will not pass you by. Your given life path and
destiny is already making its way to you. Likewise, what
is never meant for you will find a way to exit your life,
however difficult that may feel. Just know that all will
work out, clarity will come and all will make sense.
You're a tough cookie and will be ok, absolutely
brilliantly ok.

Fluorite helps you gain focus on the bigger picture and
deflect any negativity that may be blocking your true
destiny flowing to you.

#111

My past doesn't predict or define my future.

White Howlite helps release and say goodbye
to unwanted emotions and beliefs.

#112

I know my importance and worth.

Sunstone gives you a boost of confidence and empowerment as you embrace yourself for all that you are.

#113

I am learning valuable lessons from myself every day and these lessons will equip me as I face my exciting future.

Lapis lazuli opens up your inner wisdom and helps you communicate your inner truth as you strive forwards.

#114

I will rise above negative thoughts and low actions,
and they will not define my existence.

Aquamarine will have your back if you find it difficult to
express yourself as you take control of a situation.

#115

I have endless talents. Today I will utilize them
with confidence and success.

Tiger's eye awakens your confidence and belief
in yourself.

#116

I forgive those who have caused me upset in my past,
and I allow myself to peacefully detach from them.

Amethyst is a crystal of calm that allows you to move
on from past hurt and block negative vibrations
upsetting you.

#117

I am truly blessed with incredible friends and loving energy which surrounds me.

Rose Quartz attracts the very best friendships and lovers that align with you.

#118

My obstacles are moving aside and I will no longer let them stop me.

Smokey Quartz revs up your motivation to power ahead.

#119

I release my inner fears. I will conquer my demons and
rise like a phoenix.

Lava stone grounds your emotions and helps you bob
along through your day deflecting all negativity.
If you are facing a difficult time, wear lava stone.

#120

Today, I need only to focus on the right here, right now.

Carnelian helps you regain composure, remain steady and focus on the moment.

#121

Today comes with a nod to self-care and self-appreciation. It is time to spoil your beautiful soul a little more. Give yourself permission to put yourself first and allow nothing to disturb this precious time. You deserve it. Whatever it may be that makes you happy, go for it. Number 1 needs some pampering.

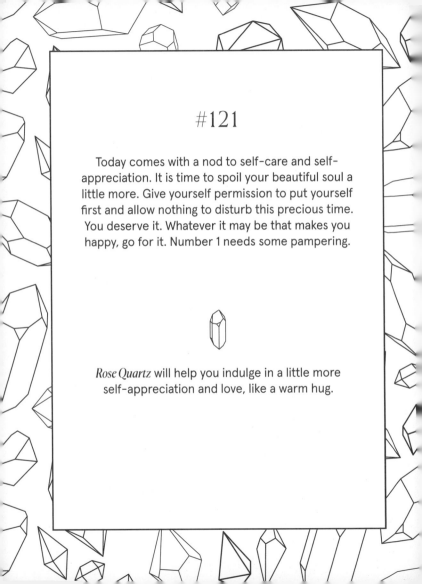

Rose Quartz will help you indulge in a little more self-appreciation and love, like a warm hug.

#122

Give yourself credit where credit is due. Step back to really appreciate how hard you work each day. Even on days you feel you've not achieved anything, you've made a difference in yours and others' lives.

Citrine helps you celebrate your beautiful soul with joy and self-appreciation.

#123

The Universe conspires to give you all that you wish
for and works alongside fate, so be sure to treat
others as you'd like to be treated. Be clear on your
wishes and desires. Whatever you project out into
the word you'll receive back tenfold. Have fun, be
kind, stay positive and remember to dream big.

Lapis lazuli is a natural filter crystal that will help
block negative energy and allow positivity to flood
into your life. It is also great for helping you trust
yourself and the process more.

#124

Fresh, green, abundant energy is surrounding you and it's time to renew your dreams and ambitions. Everything is for the taking – the key is to believe in your talents.

Fluorite helps you face the day with positivity while deflecting any negativity as you focus on your dreams.

#125

I am relaxed and calm. Calmness surrounds me as I
navigate the day ahead.

Amethyst calms your emotions ready for the day.

#126

My mind, body and spirit are my temple, and I will treat each part of me with respect by making healthy choices.

Blue lace Agate awakens your inner faith, patience and inner respect for all that you are.

#127

I will treat myself as I would a dear friend.

Rose Quartz encourages your heart chakra to open up
and let your loving energy flow in a self-caring and
nurturing way.

#128

I am excited for the day ahead.

Orange Calcite adds a little fizz into your day with a dose of sunshine and inner joy.

#129

I am open to new opportunities.

Tiger's eye brings luck and fortune to your side.

#130

I am doing my best, and that's okay.

Rose Quartz ignites self-appreciation and love.

#131

I choose to wake each morning with a smile.

Citrine awakens your inner child and happy memories.

#132

Count your lucky stars: your angels have been working
with the spirits to conjure up and manifest a very
special opportunity. It's now for you to declare that
you are ready to receive and add a new string to your
bow. Be mindful of tricksters trying to steal your
limelight, and taking credit for your achievements.
Protect your work and energy at all costs, but know
that good things are manifesting.

Manifestation Quartz lets the Universe know you
mean business.

#133

You've been working hard to manifest recently, and will be more deeply involved in whatever it is you are focused on. There is also a strong pull towards commitment at this time, and a union of like-minded minds is on the cards within the goals you have set. This may not make much sense now, but all will come together for your greatest opportunities. Your intentions have the potential to open exciting new doors.

Ocean Jasper encourages you to put energy into your manifestations and watch the magic happen.

#134

Nothing can or will stand in my way.

Garnet ignites your inner passion and determination.

#135

My confidence and self-esteem are high and
I attract more of the same.

Citrine is a master attractor of abundance that will
welcome more of the good in your life.

#136

I release what no longer serves me.

Smokey Quartz acts as a shield against unhealthy
or negative relationships and energies.

#137

Your beautiful soul deserves kind actions. Self-love and care is a must. Be kind to yourself and nourish your soul so that you can feel your best. You deserve and are allowed to be free of any difficulties or negativity in your life, even if it's only for a short while. Give yourself permission to feel joy and goodness.

Pink Tourmaline allows you to move on with self-care and love.

#138

I am adaptable, and this slight hiccup won't stop me.

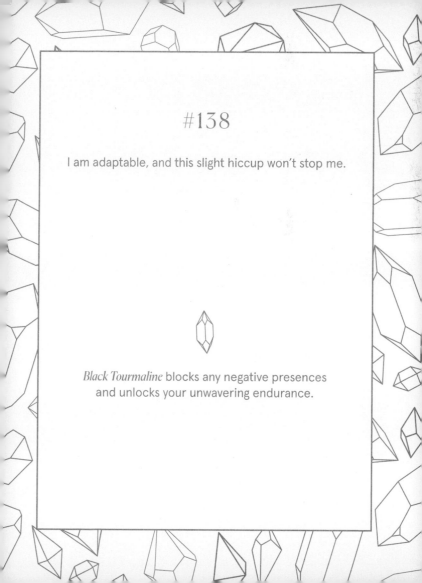

Black Tourmaline blocks any negative presences
and unlocks your unwavering endurance.

#139

It is time you believed in your incredible abilities;
you absolutely can and will succeed when you focus
your skills accordingly. Don't be afraid to seek
guidance from those you trust. Exciting times are
ahead, and just as you visualize, you are set for
bigger and brighter things.

Red Jasper empowers you with confidence and
inner strength.

#140

Numbers will be important to you. One in particular will make itself known, and this is your sign to look into its meaning. Be mindful and open to receiving the guidance from your angels and you will experience miracles and good fortune as you're guided towards your life's path in the coming months.

Amethyst helps strengthen the spiritual mind, creating a stronger connection to the spiritual and angelic realm.

#141

Doors and chapters may have closed in your life recently, so take this time to evaluate and assess your next steps. Things leave your life for a reason, making way for the bigger and better. Have the confidence to embrace the intentions you set yesterday, and set out on the path to bring them to fruition.

Green Aventurine welcomes confidence, strength and courage as you feel empowered to take action.

#142

I am proud of myself.

Tangerine Quartz invites you to self-reflect with pride, inner joy and warm emotion.

#143

I am full of joy. I feel at peace, content, motivated and I love my life.

Citrine has super energy and will help lift your self-esteem and motivation.

#144

The limits that you place on yourself are exactly that: self-limits. This spring, don't let anything get in the way of your future successes. There is an abundance of opportunities waiting for you, and gold at every turn. Open your eyes to any opportunity and make the magic happen.

Jade unlocks what exactly is holding you back.

#145

I spread light wherever I go.

Sunstone reflects your fun, contagious energy
like sunbeams.

#146

I notice the good in the world.

Labradorite awakens your inner magic to help you see
the good around you more positively.

#147

I am grounded and steady, no matter what life throws at me.

Hematite keeps your feet and emotions firmly on the ground.

#148

I am adventurous and seek out new experiences.

Golden healer Quartz awakens the adventurer within.
Let that same excitement and inquisitiveness
surface during the waking hours.

#149

There is room in my life for more joy
and abundance.

Peridot allows you to connect to more
joyful opportunities.

#150

Everyone is different: that's what makes the world go round. Exciting new discoveries happen because of different strengths and talents. This is your sign to embrace yours. Forget past judgements and allow your beautiful self to shine. Embrace your individuality and the quirks that set you apart from the next. You are a brilliant, beautiful soul, and you are loved.

Kunzite is a major healer of past trauma and setbacks that will empower you to move forwards with clarity and consideration for your true needs.

#151

I am not afraid to ask for what I need.

Sodalite helps you speak your desires and
needs with clear direction.

#152

This is your sign to appreciate you for all that you are. Self-acceptance is powerful. If only you could see how important you are to others, how much you inspire them. Work on finding the contentment in your existence, and love your beautiful soul. Look how much you do for others – they couldn't thrive without you. You're a force to be reckoned with. We value and appreciate you, and it's time you did the same.

Pink Aragonite gives you a dose of self-love and appreciation, and a reminder of your self-worth.

#153

I welcome rest, calm and stillness.

Selenite will bring a zen calmness to your surroundings.
Like a serene pond, it stills the energy, allowing you
to just be.

#154

I have grace and compassion for my mistakes.

Hematite helps you see your mistakes for exactly what they are. It grounds your emotions as you ease any associated negativity, so you can move on.

#155

A day of reflection is on the cards. Look back at the last month and ask yourself if you are on the right path or page. Is there anything that you want to change, welcome or learn? If your mind is confused or over-active, head outside and embrace the great outdoors. Your mind will be freed of noise and clarity will be restored.

Moss Agate can be carried with you to make you feel more connected to the earth and relaxed within nature.

#156

Rome wasn't built in a day, so give yourself a break. Look at how much you've achieved, reflect on all the effort you've put in and give yourself a pat on the back. Each day you strive forwards you're closer to your end goal.

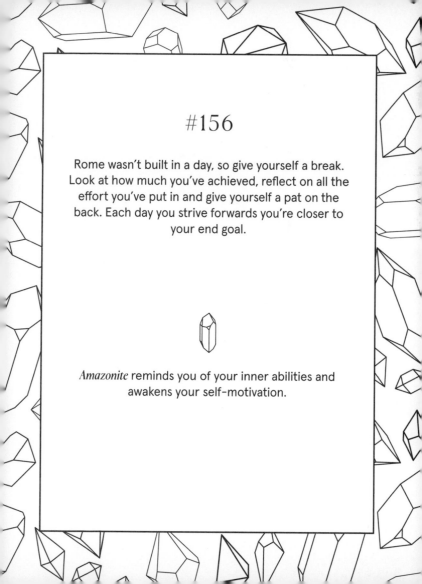

Amazonite reminds you of your inner abilities and awakens your self-motivation.

#157

I deserve freedom and peace.

Selenite welcomes zen and divine serenity
into your environment.

#158

Every action I take has a positive impact on the world.

Yellow Aventurine helps spread your motivation,
happiness and joy into the world.

#159

I have the power to make a difference in someone else's life.

Rose Quartz reminds you how loving, nurturing and caring you are to others that are fortunate enough to know you.

#160

I am responsible and trustworthy.

Blue lace Agate shines a light on the encouragement and support you show others. Refine these traits with this crystal.

#161

Failures are important lessons that you can gain wisdom from to make adjustments to your future. You have the power to use this any way you wish, and now is the time to create as many positives as you can. You are in charge of the outcome.

Black Obsidian helps you shed yourself of past regrets, and allows a beautiful new layer to shine, deflecting any negative challenges.

#162

Exciting changes are afoot. You may feel out of sorts, but know these changes are for your greater good. Embrace the new direction and path you are about to take, and allow the good to flow to you. Just plan well and take notes so you don't forget an important detail.

Pyrite attracts the most wonderful abundance into your life with clear direction.

#163

There are lots of messages crossing your path at the moment. Take on board these concerns; they are all directing you to the right path for you. Pay attention to them and you'll get the answers you want.

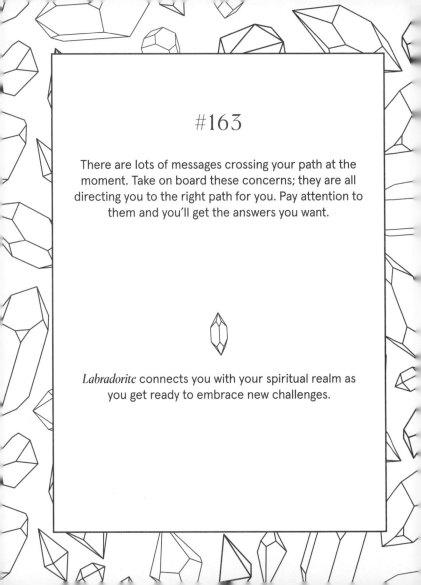

Labradorite connects you with your spiritual realm as you get ready to embrace new challenges.

#164

I am committed to making the world a better place.

Clear Quartz unlocks your crown chakra as you connect
with your divine path.

#165

Asking for help is a sign of self-respect
and self-awareness.

Lapis lazuli enhances your wisdom about
a certain situation and gives you the
confidence to ask for help.

#166

Changing my mind is a strength, not a weakness.

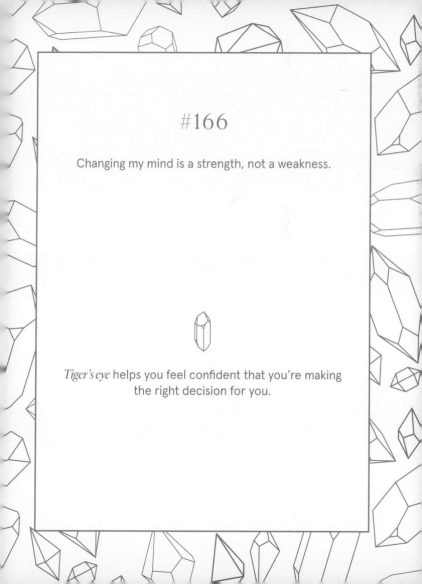

Tiger's eye helps you feel confident that you're making the right decision for you.

#167

I affirm and encourage others, as I do myself.

Smokey Quartz helps you feel secure in what you're supporting others with.

#168

Your achievements aren't going unnoticed, and you achieve anything you put your mind to. The question is: 'What next?' You've got this and have the support of your angels.

Kyanite awakens your self-belief while inviting your angels to guide you.

#169

Your strength and determination may have taken a
bit of a battering of late, but remember that you are
stronger than you could ever imagine. Use this time
to gain confidence in your abilities and remember to
take time for you. You are allowed to say no.

Moonstone invites your path of destiny to make itself
known, with a nurturing and supportive energy.

#170

I am capable of balancing ease and effort in my life.

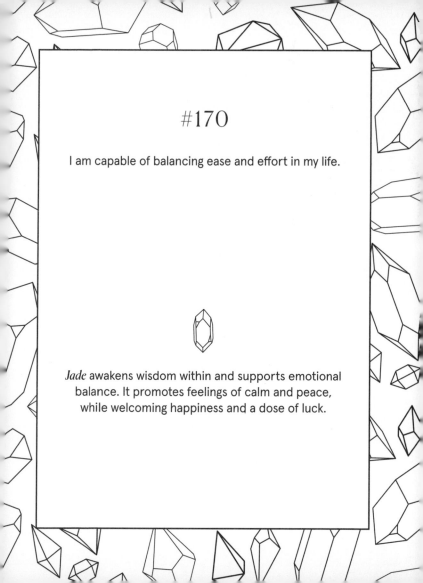

Jade awakens wisdom within and supports emotional balance. It promotes feelings of calm and peace, while welcoming happiness and a dose of luck.

#171

I am content in my existence. When I need support,
I attract the right guidance.

Rose Quartz attracts healthy, loving support networks
into your life.

#172

Happiness doesn't always rely on who you are or what you have. If you are in a difficult place emotionally, know that it is okay to feel this way. It's not permanent and you're not alone. Reach out if you need to. Trees lose their leaves every year, but they stand knowing that easier and brighter days are coming. Buds will form, flowers will bloom and new branches will grow, just like you.

Celestite welcomes calmness and peace into your environment.

#173

I am listening and am open to the messages the Universe has to offer today.

Green Aventurine attracts miracles and great opportunities with ease.

#174

I am in charge of how I feel and today I choose to
feel joy.

Dalmatian Jasper welcomes the life and emotions
you desire.

#175

I approach this new day with optimism.

Black Onyx helps you face new challenges with inner strength and a deep willpower that could rival a superhero's.

#176

If you're feeling a little lost in direction, don't dismay. Inspiration and clarity come in many ways, forms and scenarios, and you'll find yours soon. The spark will come, often in the most unusual of places. Happiness knows no bounds and you hold the key to it.

Celestite encourages openness within your energy, making you more receptive to seeing the good around you.

#177

There are new opportunities at every turn, but they are often missed. Today you are encouraged to slow down. Take stock of the details in your surroundings, the conversations around you and the moments you would otherwise have missed. As you do this, your awareness grows and you open the door to exciting new paths. Keep listening out.

Green Aventurine is a wonderful crystal for manifestation, luck and success. It will flood your life with positivity and help you to feel more grateful.

#178

I belong here and I deserve to take up space.

Red Jasper helps you introduce your true self with
confidence and own the day.

#179

I can be loving in my heart and firm in my boundaries.

Garnet welcomes exciting opportunities and
relationships with wisdom and knowledge.

#180

I can control how I respond to things.

Sodalite helps you communicate in a truthful yet considerate way.

#181

I won't pretend to be anyone or anything other than who I am.

Carnelian helps you live your life full of creativity, passion, purpose and self-love.

#182

I will attract and grow towards my interests, like
a sunflower reaching for the sun.

Green Aventurine welcomes abundance and joy into
your life.

#183

When you seek clarity to a question on your mind, give yourself permission to take time out. Allow your mind to rest so that you can be clear and work through the blocks you may have. Ask your angels for guidance through meditation.

Labradorite asks you to believe in your inner magic and trust in the messages you'll attract and receive.

#184

I have everything I need within me to succeed.

Ametrine helps you become the creator of your world.

#185

I nourish my soul with kindness and nourishing foods.

Selenite invites calm into your space for self-care and relaxation.

#186

I seek out the magic in the ordinary.

Pyrite helps manifest the most wonderful and abundant opportunities, and sparks inner joy and magic.

#187

It's time to take action. Clear out any clutter, leave old grievances behind and turn over a fresh page. When one door closes, another more bountiful one can open. Start the emotional clear-out today. It will be worth it.

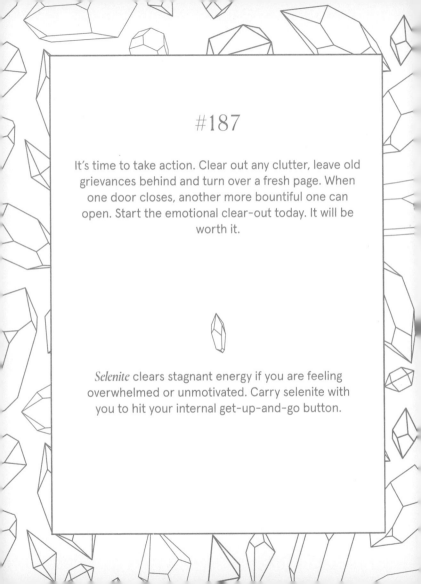

Selenite clears stagnant energy if you are feeling overwhelmed or unmotivated. Carry selenite with you to hit your internal get-up-and-go button.

#188

Your angels are around you more than ever right now.
They're with you as you make decisions, and work with
crystals and the Universe for your greater good. Feel
their warm energy as you celebrate today. You're
loved, important and very special indeed.

Mookaite Jasper reminds you that the Universe is ready
and prepared to guide you

#189

It's time to trust your abilities more and give yourself the confidence to deal with anything the day brings. Everyday you continue to grow, evolve and develop into a stronger and wiser person. Today, have fun, because you are pure magic.

Hematite will keep your emotions and energy grounded. It will keep your mind on task and you motivated on your goals when you feel overwhelmed.

#190

I am aligned with the cycles of the seasons and attract
their energies in abundance.

Aura Quartz activates the light within to work with the
energies of the environment.

#191

I will not silence my truth, as my truth should
be heard.

Amazonite empowers you to speak your inner worth
from your highest truth.

#192

I allow myself to evolve and move on from past hurt.

Rose Quartz helps diminish feelings of guilt when you are moving on from a situation for your better self.

#193

I am not in competition with anyone else, including myself. I will focus on my successes and my own story.

Amazonite reminds you how incredible you are. Not only will it help you focus on all that you need within, but it will boost your motivation.

#194

Personal or professional relationships will be the focus of the day. Someone you've had issue with may be a little more on edge than usual, so it's best to approach any meeting with a deep breath and clear mind. Remember, you're not the product of someone else's opinions or energy.

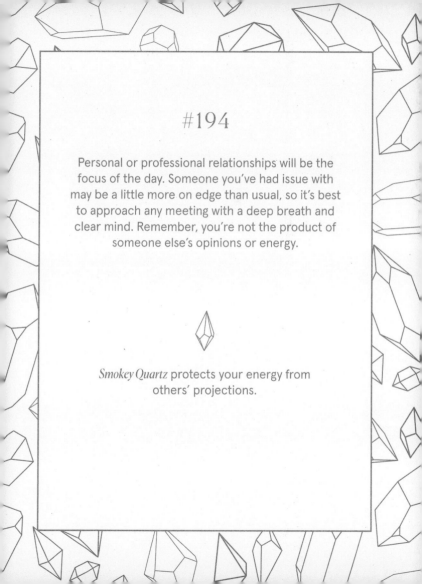

Smokey Quartz protects your energy from others' projections.

#195

Each day is exactly what you make it. If you're feeling a little blue or anxious, remember that you control the narrative. There are thousands of other opportunities out there for you. It's for you to go and find them.

Pyrite attracts the very best of what is meant for you.

#196

There is no growth in stillness. I will flourish and
grow each and every day.

Green Aventurine is a powerful attractor of abundant
opportunities. Use this crystal to guide you along
your chosen life path.

#197

I can change my mind at any turn. It's my choice.

Amethyst reduces anxiety and helps you think with more clarity about the next step.

#198

When I forgive myself, I free myself.

Clear Quartz allows deep inner healing and helps you feel the pure, beautiful light that is radiating from you.

#199

When I speak my needs and desires, I will receive
them abundantly.

Blue Moonstone helps you manifest anything you
desire and abundant opportunities.

#200

Nature is calling. Take time to be at one with your beautiful green surroundings, be it a tree, field or potted plants on a window sill. Relax your shoulders, unclench your jaw, take a deep breath and let out a big sigh. Feel your muscles unwind as you appreciate the natural forces around you.

Ammonite helps your energy connect with that of nature, helping both flow together.

#201

It's time to be honest. Something has been troubling
you but you are feeling indecisive about your inner
feelings and what they really mean. Your mind is
clouded. Allow yourself to stop and focus: trust in your
inner intuition and gut instinct. You may well have
been subconsciously creating blocks, but know that
this will just pave over the truth. You know what you
need – go with your soul's most pressing needs and
desires and you'll feel as free as a bird.

Fluorite eases any stresses and inspires you to focus
your vision and aspirations on your next step.

#202

Everyone is different! That's what makes the world go round. Exciting new happenings and discoveries occur because of different strengths and talents. Embrace your individuality, your beliefs and style, and the quirks that set you apart. You're loved and a brilliant, shining beautiful soul.

Moldavite helps you embrace your limitless spirit and attract your path of destiny with determination.

#203

It's okay to change direction. It's okay not to have all your ducks in a row. It's okay to have a new opinion of something or someone. It's okay to try something new. Listen to your intuition and go for it.

Carnelian enhances confidence, lights a fire within and gives strength.

#204

I feel good about myself and I am kind to myself.

Azurite helps you feel content with your existence and
see your positives as others do.

#205

I believe in my ability to achieve anything.

Jade brings luck to your side as you work towards achieving your goals.

#206

Feed your mind and soul with positive words, intentions and thoughts. How you talk to yourself has a huge impact on your wellbeing, so it's time to remind yourself to be kind. Your greatest relationship is with yourself. Write down words and thoughts that awaken your happiness and make you smile on paper to refer back to. You are allowed to be happy. You are in charge of your existence.

Rose Quartz helps you appreciate yourself for all that you are.

#207

I let my feelings flow freely without any fear.

Sodalite helps you communicate clearly with less stress
and anxiety as you speak your truth.

#208

I inhale confidence and self-love and
exhale self-doubt.

Malachite welcomes inner growth and
positive challenges with confidence.

#209

My struggles are my opportunities to prosper, earn and grow.

Carnelian activates your sacral chakra and ignites your deep inner confidence to see the bigger picture.

#210

I love the person I am.

Rose Quartz invites you to bathe in its pink glow
to see the loving soul that others see.

#211

Take some time out for you today. No matter how
long or short, it's important to give yourself a
breather. Some time to think, some time to assess,
some time to just be. Play your favourite song, read
a book, feel the ground on the soles of your feet,
feel the wind in your hair, reconnect with nature and
feel the serenity. It's not selfish to take time for you;
it will help you be the best version of yourself.

Amethyst encourages you to take a breather and allow
calm to wash over you.

#212

So many have benefited from your kind words,
gestures and loving guidance these last few months.
In return, good fortune in abundance is flowing your
way. Watch out for those amazing opportunities as
you go about your day over the next few weeks.

Turquenite helps you celebrate your successes and
attract more of the same.

#213

I say no to toxic people and situations with ease.

Black Onyx promotes stamina and strength during times of stress, confusion and unease.

#214

I let go of my past and joyously live in the present.

Carnelian ignites the self-belief within to light up
your courage and wisdom.

#215

Today is rich with opportunities and I open myself to receiving them.

Tiger's eye attracts good fortune and positive opportunities.

#216

I don't worry about things I can't control. I trust that
everything will work out for my wellbeing.

Black Obsidian banishes any negative thoughts
and transmutes them to positivity.

#217

It's lovely that you're kind and supportive of others,
but it's just as important – if not more so – to be
kind and supportive of yourself. Speak kindly of your
talents, skills and abilities. Accept compliments, look
in the mirror and be proud of all that you are:
a beautiful, kind human being.

Rhodonite raises your spirits and awakens a warm,
nurturing inner energy.

#218

Your angels, crystals and the Universe can see you
putting the hard work in to manifest your dreams,
goals and desires, and are sending luck and self-belief
your way to help you fulfil and receive them. Imagine
stardust falling around you and give thanks for all the
amazing things about to come your way.

Jade is a crystal of good fortune and luck that will
work in your favour.

#219

Something amazing is on the horizon. You may not be
aware of change manifesting, but you will be faced
with an incredible opportunity in the coming weeks.
Just open your eyes a little more to see the clues
around you. There could also be more responsibility
at work, or a new income stream if you want to
welcome it. Embrace the good thatis happening.

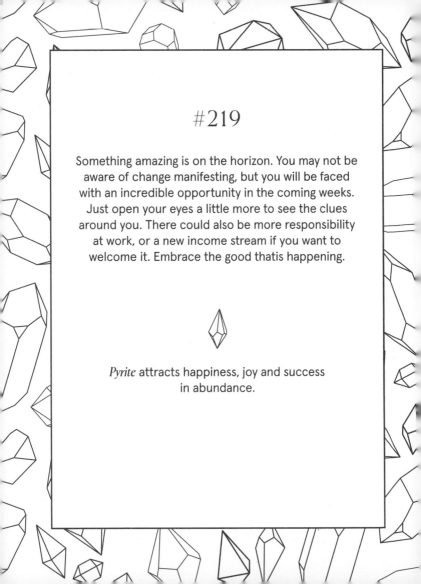

Pyrite attracts happiness, joy and success
in abundance.

#220

You were born for big and bright things. Self-belief is
what you need; just remember that if someone else
has achieved it, so can you.

Orange Agate spurs on your self-belief for motivation
when needed.

#221

Listen out for words of wisdom from unexpected sources. Something that's been weighing on your mind isn't as troublesome as you initially thought, and these words could offer a resolution to take the weight off your shoulders. All will be settled soon, bringing a level of contentment.

Lepidolite connects to your third eye to activate receiving messages from the divine or someone you care about.

#222

I am in tune with my destiny and the infinite possibilities of my existence.

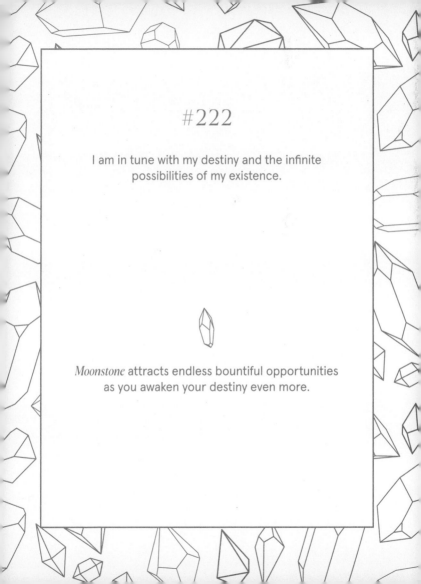

Moonstone attracts endless bountiful opportunities as you awaken your destiny even more.

#223

The more I learn, the more I achieve.

Fluorite helps you stay focused on the task in hand.

#224

I am determined to get the best out of my day.

Carnelian ignites your inner desires and motivation.

#225

Hard work will lead to me living my dreams.

Clear Quartz awakens your focus with clarity so
you can see the next steps you need to take.

#226

I bring light with me wherever I go.

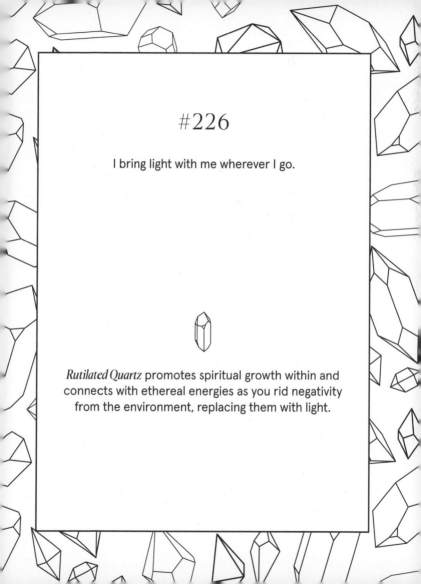

Rutilated Quartz promotes spiritual growth within and connects with ethereal energies as you rid negativity from the environment, replacing them with light.

#227

I manifest and attract reasons to be happy.

Citrine creates an aura of sparkles and sunshine
as you enlighten the lives of those you meet and
attract miracles into your life.

#228

Actions speak louder than words and persistence is
the key to my success.

Bronzite helps you navigate any challenges and attack
tasks like a warrior.

#229

You may be tempted to splash the cash on a big purchase, but think about it overnight and check the small print to be sure you have covered all bases. When you do so, you'll benefit greatly. Excitement is en route for you and a loved one.

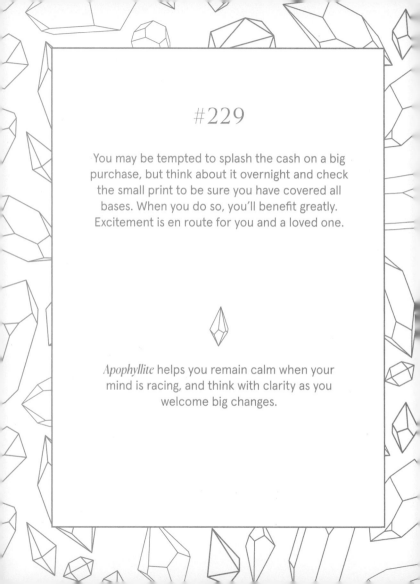

Apophyllite helps you remain calm when your mind is racing, and think with clarity as you welcome big changes.

#230

I am in charge of my energy and joy is my vibe.

Red Aventurine awakens your inner joy and helps
you work through trust issues with confidence.

#231

My sadness does not define me.

Turritella Agate activates your survival instincts
during difficult times. Strength and protection
are on your side.

#232

I am not alone with my feelings because many
experience them too.

Amber Aragonite teaches you to trust and process
your feelings and be aware of any emotions that
come with them.

#233

I am proud of how I am about to get through this day.

Flower Agate helps you feel grounded and to welcome new beginnings, transformation and growth with clarity.

#234

I am valuable even when I am not productive.

Plum blossom Jasper promotes your inner feelings of safety, security and stability. Be happy exactly where you are.

#235

You have what it takes to take that next step and move forwards. Take the kernels of wisdom from your past experience and make any personal shifts to ensure that history won't repeat itself. If positive growth can come out of the past painful chapter, then that's a win.

Blue Quartz alleviates any fears and empowers you to grow with creativity.

#236

The tools I need to succeed are in my possession.

Tiger's eye helps you feel empowered by your talents.

#237

I am a winner.

Honey Calcite helps you look at your existence with
gratitude for all that you have.

#238

Everything will work out for me.

Yellow Jasper raises your self-awareness and
self-belief in a nurturing way.

#239

There is nobody better to get the job done than me.

Rutilated Quartz helps you start the day with immense willpower and determination.

#240

You deserve every ounce of happiness that's in your life, and there's even more around the corner. Don't try hard to look for it; new happiness will flood in your life when you least expect it.

Yellow Topaz attracts an abundance of sunshine into your life.

#241

It can sometimes be difficult but try not to allow anyone to devalue you or your worth. Remember: you are bigger, better and more capable than you can imagine. You are a different person to each and every person who knows you based on their beliefs and opinions of the world, and only you know the real you. Be authentic to your dreams and concentrate on your own happiness.

Mangano Calcite welcomes deep inner peace and healing, and allows positive, loving energy to flood within.

#242

Happiness is within my grasp.

Pink Opal banishes negativity to allow compassion,
happiness and love in.

#243

I am confident in the presence of others.

Red Tiger's eye awakens your confidence and gives you the strength to deal with difficult personalities.

#244

I have confidence in my skills.

Ruby helps you feel grounded and to trust in your
ability to cope and succeed.

#245

I will say no when I don't have the time or inclination to act.

Black Tourmaline calms any negative emotions that come with a difficult situation.

#246

The success of others will not make me jealous. My time will come.

Calcopyrite helps you remain calm and loyal to the cause, and invigorated and inspired by the success of others.

#247

The only person who can defeat me is myself.

Red Jasper helps you gain empowerment from within your root chakra and awakens your inner strength and confidence.

#248

Today is full of joyful gratitude and honest reflection, and this is your sign to write down all that you are grateful for. It is the little details that make life rich. Shout out loud one thing that brings you joy, right now.

Citrine cultivates your inner sunshine and optimism, helping you see everything for what it really is.

#249

Like a moth to a flame, it's easy to be drawn to the bright lights and sparkles. But it's important to look over the situation, take a step back and offer yourself the advice you would offer to a friend. You will know what you need to do.

Lepidolite connects you with your inner guidance and angels to bring yourself back to the now.

#250

This is temporary. I have felt this before and
I was fine.

Amethyst calms any nerves and worries as you face the
day or situation ahead.

#251

I am calm. I am collected. I am in control.

Selenite helps regain your zen composure and the serenity around you.

#252

I breathe in calm and feel my tension melting away.

Amethyst is the crystal of calm and relaxation and has
a similar soothing effect on the senses as lavender.

#253

A lucky streak is heading your way. The excitement
is building and you will receive some unexpected
news, and maybe even a small windfall. Take that
chance you've been considering as it's going to
pay off and more! If this doesn't make sense right
now, it will all become clear in due course. Good
fortune is headed towards you.

Tiger's eye welcomes and attracts luck, good fortune
and success.

#254

Change and excitement will start entering your life today without causing upset and chaos. Follow your intuition, especially in relationships where you can take a chance to break the ice. Chance encounters are possible and you will be attracted to unusual types of people.

Clear Quartz connects you to your intuition with clear direction and clarity.

#255

I am valuable to the world and everyone that I meet.

Red Jasper will ignite your self-worth and self-esteem
and let your true self radiate.

#256

Happiness is achieved when you stop waiting for it and make the most of the moment you are in now. No matter how small, start making things happen now.

Green Aventurine is known for its get-up-and-go energy, and will help you feel inspired to get the ball rolling.

#257

My commitment to improving myself is real.

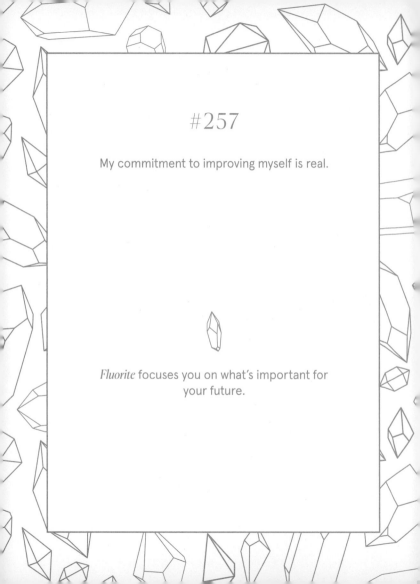

Fluorite focuses you on what's important for your future.

#258

Positivity is a choice I choose to make.

Orange Agate reminds you that darker days will pass
and ignites your inner joy.

#259

I choose hope over fear.

Aquamarine surrounds you with courage
and protection.

#260

I do not need others for my own happiness.

Rhodochrosite helps you feel a deep inner love
and self-appreciation.

#261

Your beautiful soul needs nourishment. This is your sign to embark on meditation; take some deep breaths and spend some time on your hobby or in nature. Your soul will then feel contented and at ease.

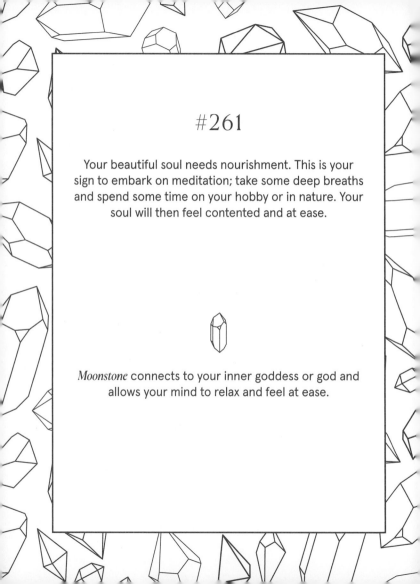

Moonstone connects to your inner goddess or god and allows your mind to relax and feel at ease.

#262

I inhale peace. I exhale anxiety or stress.

Amethyst can be held while repeating this affirmation to invite calm into your life.

#263

Persistence is key when you are working towards an end goal. There will be days when you feel like walking away, but stick with it. The hurdles are worth jumping over to gain the success you've only ever dreamt of. Your goals are within reach.

Bloodstone gives you the motivation to persevere and find the courage, no matter what.

#264

Take time today to ground, cleanse and restore your energy. Feel your feet root to the ground. Look after you so that you can continue to be the angel you are.

Prehnite with Epidote protects your emotions and prevents others' negative vibes and trauma from weighing on your shoulders.

#265

I am free of worry and am at peace with my decisions.
There is no wrong decision. I trust in the direction I
choose to take.

Sapphire reminds you that peace and fulfilment are
yours for the taking.

#266

I have a unique set of talents and I will see this project
or situation through with ease. I will succeed.

Carnelian reminds you that nothing will stand in
your way.

#267

My thoughts are kind to me because I deserve
inner peace.

Pearl provides a calming effect that will bring peace
to an overactive mind.

#268

I respect my body and listen to its needs.

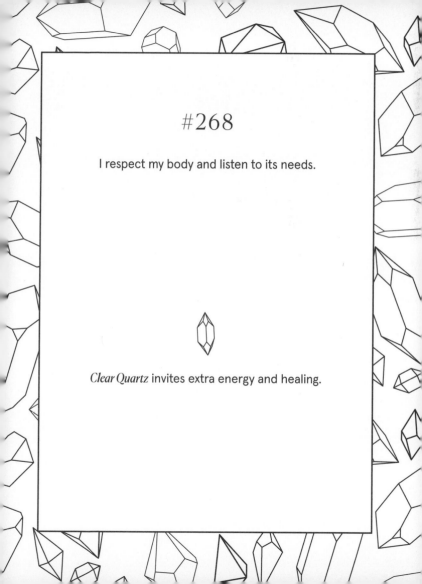

Clear Quartz invites extra energy and healing.

#269

Love, luck and joyful energies have been sent by your angels and are ready to work for you. If you don't yet feel their benefits, close your eyes and visualize pink, green and golden colours around you like an aura glow. Imagine green near your head, pink near your chest and gold near your stomach.

Chakra jewellery will help you to work with each specific energy need.

#270

My feelings are just as valid as anyone else's.

Rhodochrosite encourages you to give yourself a big dose of self-acceptance and to accept yourself for exactly who you are.

#271

I am a good person who deserves good things.

Jade attracts good fortune and lucky opportunities.

#272

The Universe sends me guidance when I
need uplifting.

Labradorite ignites your spiritual awareness
to connect.

#273

Life is guiding and flowing through me. I trust life.

Blue Calcite helps to create natural flow within
your life.

#274

I am a beautiful person.

Rose Quartz welcomes self-love into your life and
helps you appreciate yourself for all you are.

#275

Let your emotions flow. Scream, cry, laugh,
shout, jump up and down, shake your arms and
let all that energy out. Feeling your emotions
and addressing them will release your tension
and allow you to move on.

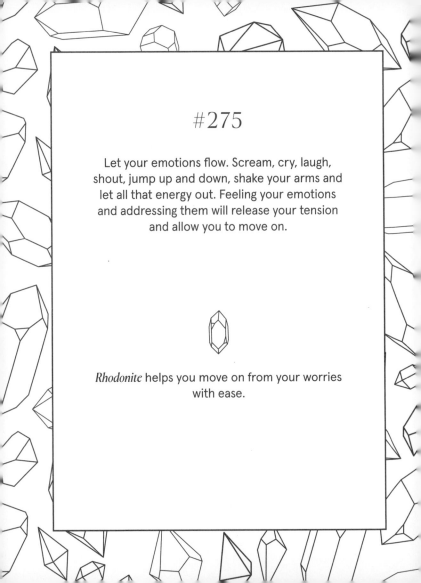

Rhodonite helps you move on from your worries
with ease.

#276

My spirit feels free and light, and I know what I
need to do.

Citrine boosts your self-confidence and self-esteem
as you embark on your new chapter.

#277

Your destiny has been mapped out for you, so trust the process that you and the Universe are creating. If you're feeling stressed and your intuition is telling you something is wrong, it's time to take a look at the wider picture to see what needs to change.

Sodalite promotes good communication and better decision making, and calms nerves.

#278

I am on the best path for me.

Hematite attracts your destiny and any prophecies.

#279

My goals are getting closer to completion every day.

Ruby celebrates your small wins as you build your
dreams with confidence.

#280

Be kind and focus on love, your hobbies and those things that make you smile. It's time to realign your needs and concentrate on the things that make you feel good. Give more time to those and you will reap the benefits emotionally, physically and mentally.

Rose Quartz attracts love wherever you go.

#281

I will master distractions and keep my focus
on my goals.

Fluorite gets you back in the zone when you
feel yourself wavering.

#282

The little things in my life make all the difference.

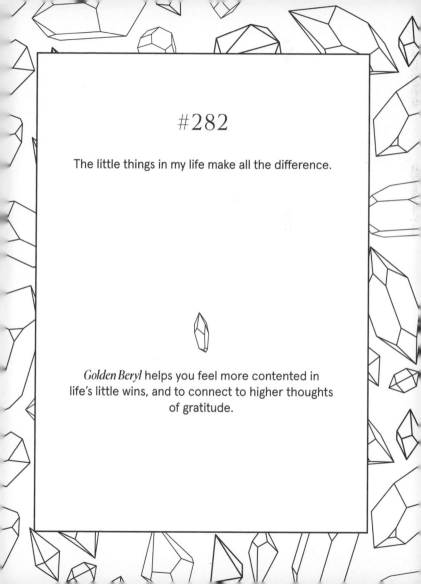

Golden Beryl helps you feel more contented in life's little wins, and to connect to higher thoughts of gratitude.

#283

My inner fears and self-deprecation diminish as I live
my life with acceptance and courage.

Black Obsidian will block, banish, absorb and transform
ill feelings towards yourself so you can see yourself for
the incredible person you truly are.

#284

My strength is stronger than my anxiety.

Red Jasper empowers you to feel confident in your
inner strength as you face the day.

#285

Use your intuition wisely. Crystals and angels have your
back, but your inner guide is just as powerful. Take
a step back to look at a situation that's troubled you.
You have the ability to gain clarity; just take your time.

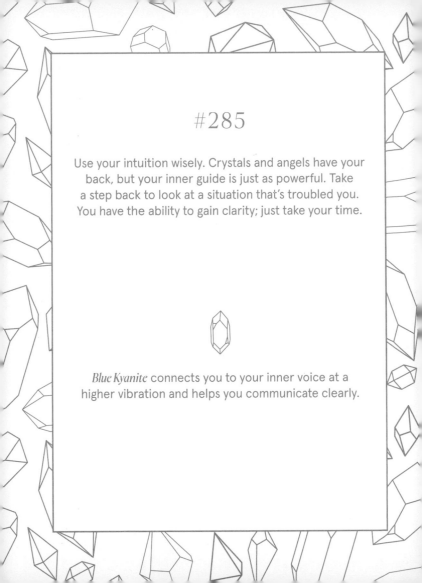

Blue Kyanite connects you to your inner voice at a
higher vibration and helps you communicate clearly.

#286

I move beyond stress to peace.

Peridot helps you feel in control as you take the next
steps towards feeling relaxed and at peace.

#287

My feelings are not facts. I will not make a hasty decision while feeling overwhelmed or not in a balanced place.

Fluorite helps clear an overwhelmed mind, and to gain focus when needed.

#288

My inner child is happy and fulfilled. I allow myself to experience joy and fun.

Dalmatian Jasper allows childlike joy to flood into your life.

#289

I will let go of 'what ifs'.

Orange Calcite helps you feel confident in
your next move.

#290

An opportunity is upon you. Open that door wide and take the opportunity. You may be worried, but listen to the details, mull it over and don't be afraid to ask questions. Fun times are ahead.

Green Aventurine attracts good and healthy opportunities.

#291

I respond to difficulties in life with calm and grace.

Yellow Jasper helps you stay in control with positivity.

#292

I am more capable than I give myself credit for.
I am talented and can achieve exactly what I put
my mind to.

Rose Quartz awakens your self-belief.

#293

My strength knows no bounds. I can and will get through this.

Garnet helps you feel grounded and empowered for your next move.

#294

Everyone deserves love in their life; the most important relationship is the one you have with yourself. You are worthy of your greatest love.

Rose Quartz will give you loving energy and nurture your self-love radar, attracting loving opportunities and plenty of calm and zen.

#295

Balance in life is what I strive for.

Petalite helps you regain harmony and balance
between the mind, body and spirit.

#296

I will take time to put myself first. My needs are as important as others'.

Tangerine Quartz quashes any feelings of guilt as you put yourself first.

#297

There could be a new individual heading into your life, making you feel a little threatened. Instead of feeling like you'll be passed by, try to use their knowledge to further yours. Don't be afraid to ask for guidance or extra training. Be inspired to become an even better version of the amazing person you are now.

Black Obsidian transmutes any negatives into positives for your greater good.

#298

My progress is always moving forwards. Success is on the horizon.

Pyrite helps you feel sunshine, motivation and empowerment as you attract abundance.

#299

I am a positive influence and I surround myself
with like-minded individuals.

Rose Quartz attracts healthy, positive relationships.

#300

Balance is key. I will mix self-care with effort.

Clear Quartz clears your mind and welcomes balance,
as you gain the physical energy to make the changes
you desire.

#301

I believe in the power of positive thinking. Good things
will flow to me as I attract like for like.

Citrine attracts success, opportunities, good deals,
money and feelings of happiness.

#302

Everyone deserves to feel nurtured and loved, especially you. Close your eyes and imagine beautiful pink, mellow and soothing energy hugging you with warmth. Let your worries drift away from your existence. Allow the pink energy to surround you like candyfloss and say out loud: 'I am loving, I am loved'.

Mangano Calcite welcomes a warm hug into your energy field.

#303

When opportunity knocks, I will open the door without hesitation.

Smokey Quartz banishes any negative thoughts and welcomes fame and success.

#304

Stay focused on the signs and synchronicities happening around you. The numbers you keep seeing aren't just coincidence. Look up their angel meaning for a deep hidden message that you need to hear.

Aura Quartz helps you gain a deeper connection to your angel and divine guides.

#305

Money spent comes back to me multiplied.

Citrine is known as the money magnet. Place it in your
wallet or purse to attract money in abundance.

#306

Without you, the world wouldn't sparkle half as much. You have instrumented monumental changes in both yours and others' lives. Now focus that sparkle on the next chapter in your life. So much good is coming your way.

Amethyst helps you stay level-headed with less stress as you navigate exciting changes.

#307

I am strong, capable and resilient. I am determined to build the life that I aspire to. I deserve the best.

Leopardskin Jasper brings strength, stability and calm to chaotic situations.

#308

I am deserving of genuine friendships and love. I am
loved and I love everything about my beautiful self.

Garnet invites unconditional love and friendships into
your life.

#309

I am ready to let go of what no longer brings me joy and ignites my passion. I welcome the new waves of excitement in abundance.

Manifestation Quartz welcomes your true desires and dreams.

#310

I am ready for a new start. I have so many new opportunities ahead of me and I am now ready to grow.

Hematite helps you get unstuck from current situations and move on with strength.

#311

Your intuition doesn't lie. If you are feeling
unsure about your next move, revisit it later.
Deep down, though, we feel you already know
what you need to do. Have more self-belief, as
your angels believe in you.

Garden Quartz helps you work with your higher
realm to gain clarity with regards to your intuition.

#312

All that I desire is manifesting. I am grateful for the
abundance flowing my way.

Emerald stimulates the free flow of money towards
your bank account.

#313

I am empowered to live, learn and grow. My challenges are opportunities that will feed me wisdom.

Malachite absorbs all of the knowledge you've been given and stimulates your mind as you continue to learn.

#314

I attract my dream opportunities and experiences with ease.

Tiger's eye attracts good luck, fortune and prosperity.

#315

I attract the energy I need to transform. I trust the process.

Tourmalinated Quartz opens you up to receive all the tools you need to move forwards.

#316

Believe in yourself, your skills, talents and abilities a
little bit more. You are more than capable to set the
wheels in motion or to finish the project on your
mind. We empower you to just go for it. What's the
worst that could happen? You'll be in exactly the
same position you are now. The best? You'd have
moved on or completed whatever is on your mind.
Start the day as you mean to go on.

Red Jasper boosts your motivation and gives you the
physical stamina to achieve exactly what you need.

#317

Start the project, have the conversation, show your true feelings, research that trip. Follow the dreams and passions that ignite your soul. Fun is on the horizon.

Carnelian fires up your motivation. Let nothing stand in your way.

#318

I am thankful for all that I have received and all that
is to be delivered to me from the seeds I have sown.
I am ready.

Moonstone helps you birth successful new ideas.

#319

I can and will express my feelings with confidence and truth.

Sodalite helps you communicate your truths and deep feelings with confidence.

#320

I am full of energy and optimism. I will practice self-care when needed without guilt.

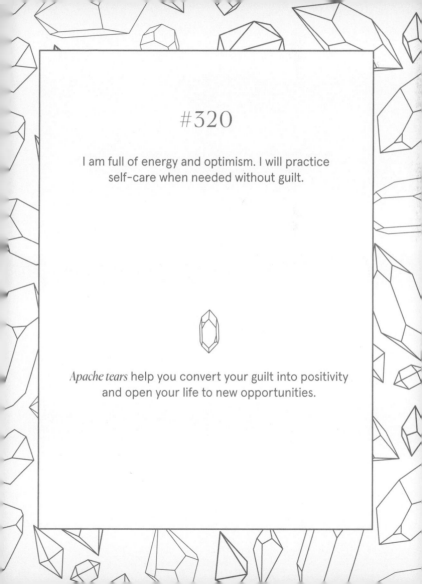

Apache tears help you convert your guilt into positivity and open your life to new opportunities.

#321

Change is my friend. I do not fear it.

Hematite grounds and harmonizes your emotions as
you navigate the changes in your life.

#322

Your angels want you to know that all of your
efforts don't go unnoticed. They are proud of all
of the adventures you've faced, the lessons you've
learned and the wisdom you now utilize as you go
along your life's path. Keep shining. You should be
so proud of yourself.

Garden Quartz connects you with your higher and
angelic realm.

#323

Love, friendship and relationships in general may have been a little bothersome recently, but loving energy is shining around you right now. The greatest love story you can have is with yourself, so practice some self-compassion today.

Rose Quartz surrounds you with loving and nurturing energy.

#324

It's okay to let go of what no longer serves you, or that doesn't bring positivity into your life. There is power in walking away from situations that no longer bring you joy.

Black Tourmaline protects and grounds your energy to give you time to process and heal.

#325

I attract positive energy like a magnet.

Citrine attracts joy, abundance and the motivation to complete your goals.

#326

Everything that needs to get done will get done, and it's okay to ask for help.

Lapis lazuli helps you seek out the wisdom to find the answers you need.

#327

Today and every day, I am blessed.

Celestite opens you up to more blessings and
angelic guidance.

#328

I trust my inner wisdom and make confident decisions.

Iolite helps you to gain confidence and clarity regarding what is on your mind, and to trust in yourself more.

#329

I release the past and embrace the present.

Rhodonite helps you let go of long-held trauma and upset and heal.

#330

It's time for you to regain your life and soul energy to feel the best you can and be doused in happiness. If something makes you feel bad, you owe it nothing.

Smokey Quartz helps you dispel negativity and attract abundance and happiness.

#331

I am understood and my perspective is important.

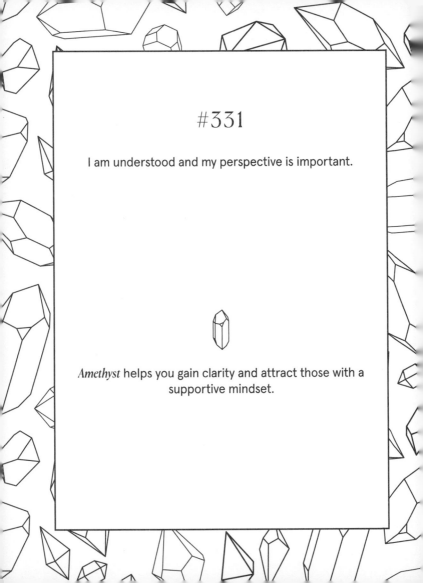

Amethyst helps you gain clarity and attract those with a
supportive mindset.

#332

I am still learning, so it's okay to make mistakes.

Black Obsidian transmutes any worries and empowers you with new wisdom.

#333

I am worthy of investing in myself.

Carnelian raises your sense of power, confidence and courage.

#334

Your lost loved ones are never far away. Your memories, conversations and tributes don't go unnoticed. Keep their light burning. Know that when you call on them, they hear you, and will leave you signs when you least expect them. You are loved and are cheered on every step of the way.

Angelite awakens your connection to your angels and allows them to hear you clearly.

#335

I am proud of how far I have come and look forward
to applying the wisdom I have gained, daily.

Lapis lazuli helps you hold on to the wisdom you
have gained.

#336

I embrace spontaneity.

Labradorite encourages you to embrace the magic in the air and follow the excitement.

#337

I make time to process my emotions when needed.
I won't be rushed into anything until I am ready. I
deserve to heal.

Rhodonite helps you heal and move on with
self-kindness and awareness.

#338

Self-care is important right now and it's okay to put your needs first. Give yourself permission to take time for you, no matter how short or long.

Clear Quartz helps you tune in to your divine energy and true needs.

#339

You deserve to live the life of your dreams. Remember, you can and will make the changes you desire! In the meantime, get the ball rolling with one project today. There's no time like the present to make things happen. Trust your skills and abilities to get you there.

Citrine attracts your desires and gives you confidence to follow up and chase what you need.

#340

Adventures are coming! It's time to have faith in the new opportunity put your way. Large or small, it will set you out of your comfort zone and help you grow as a person in strength and confidence. This will give you the tools to keep progressing with success on your life's path.

Rainbow Moonstone attracts positive new opportunities and beginnings.

#341

My body is beautiful in this current moment, shape and size.

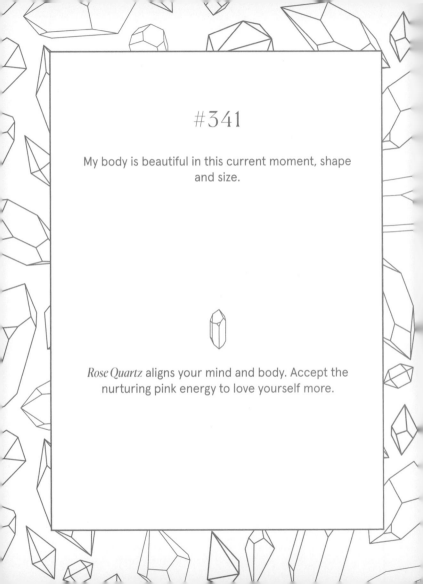

Rose Quartz aligns your mind and body. Accept the nurturing pink energy to love yourself more.

#342

I am worthy of feeling good, looking good, dressing
well and treating myself.

Red Jade awakens the warrior within you. Show the
world your passion and what you are truly made of.

#343

I allow myself to rest. I am a work in progress and progress needs time out, too.

Amethyst allows you to relax. Keep it close by to help your muscles unwind. Pop it in the bath with you for ultimate relaxation.

#344

There is something in the world that only I can do,
and that's why I am here.

Celestite connects you to your divine and aligns you
with your soul purpose.

#345

You have the strength to deal with whatever
challenges life sends your way. They are tests to
raise you even higher, for each and every time you
defeat a situation, you grow in energy and resilience.
Look in the mirror and remind yourself exactly who
you are. Know that the spirit is with you at every step,
guiding and supporting you towards even bigger
and brighter opportunities.

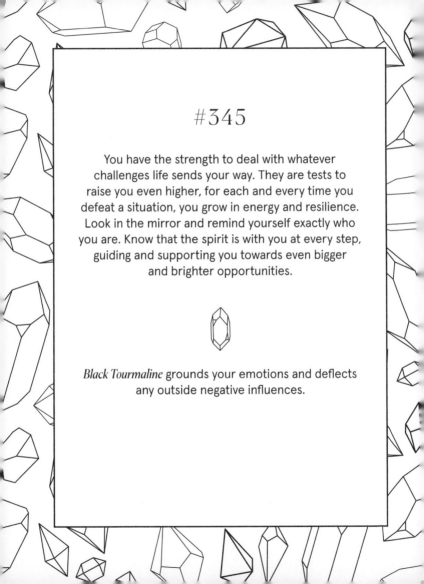

Black Tourmaline grounds your emotions and deflects
any outside negative influences.

#346

Your angels and spirit guides are aware that something is on your mind. They have been by your side more than usual and have been sending signs to give you the answer you've been craving. Follow your intuition and be open-minded. All will become clear, but for now, ask them for guidance and trust in your own abilities to make things happen.

Blue lace Agate helps you reach the higher spiritual realms and clears the path to communication with your angels.

#347

Start honouring your promises to yourself and do one thing today for you. You're just as important as those you love or the things you are tasked to do, if not more so.

Carnelian ignites your motivation and confidence.

#348

You may feel a little emotionally wounded of late.
Cross words may have been spoken or jealous minds
may be at play. Know that when you focus on your
path, and not the opinions of others, you allow your
wings to grow and flourish. Concentrate on all the
wondrous things in your life and act with gratitude. You
will welcome more light and love into your existence,
and anger and jealousy will cease to affect you.

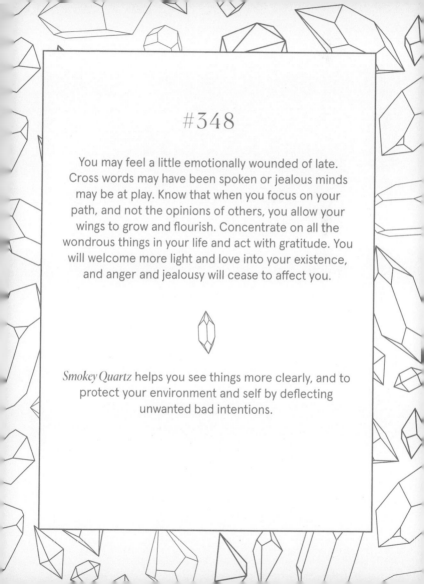

Smokey Quartz helps you see things more clearly, and to
protect your environment and self by deflecting
unwanted bad intentions.

#349

Imagine a bubble of grounding energy surrounding you or a loved one. Visualize transmuting any dark vibes by turning them into light. See the light radiating from you. Accept and receive this energy to empower you through any situation you may need support with right now.

Hematite helps you feel more grounded and protected.

#350

When I talk to myself as I would a friend, I see all my best qualities and I allow myself to shine.

Mangano Calcite helps you spread kindness wherever you go. Most importantly, this crystal will enable you to see you for the fabulous person you are.

#351

Kindness is my nature, but I ensure it's protected from those who wish me harm.

Clear Quartz allows the light energy to fill your aura and deflect any negativity.

#352

I've got this, and nothing can hold me back.

Tiger's eye helps you focus. When making a decision, carry this crystal with you as you head through an important day.

#353

Challenges are lessons and I learn from them with ease.

Lapis lazuli unlocks your inner wisdom to help you make wise decisions.

#354

Emotions may be heightened today. Difficult decisions need to be made for good or hard reasons, but they need to be made. Things will feel better once you've made a focused plan, and this will give you the strength to move forwards.

Red Jasper helps you stay grounded and level-headed, and to realize your inner strength.

#355

Count your lucky stars by making the effort to practice gratitude today. Look around you and choose three things you are thankful for. Make your list, give thanks and enjoy the sunny feeling it gives you. Practice gratitude to welcome more abundance into your life, for a positive attitude welcomes a positive life.

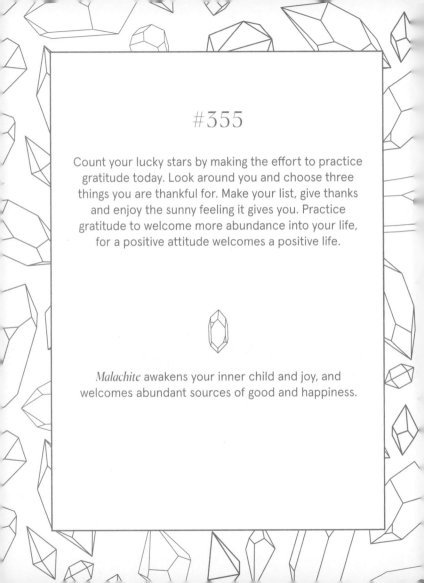

Malachite awakens your inner child and joy, and welcomes abundant sources of good and happiness.

#356

Inspiring greatness in others is my calling. I uplift and
motivate those around me.

Amethyst will help you realize your inner goals.

#357

I am the writer of my own story and the master of my own path.

Clear Quartz connects you with your soul purpose.

#358

Communication is key today. Although you may find it hard to converse with those you don't know very well, it's important you try, as this could open new opportunities for you. Luck is on your side today and your favourite colour could be key.

Sodalite helps you talk freely, openly and with purpose.

#359

I choose to surround myself with positive and loving people. These people will help me grow mentally, physically and spiritually.

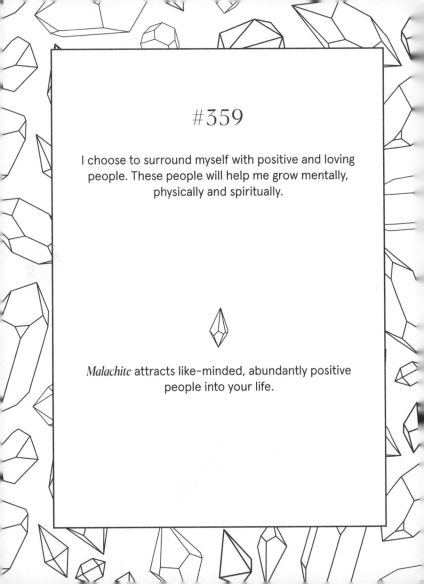

Malachite attracts like-minded, abundantly positive people into your life.

#360

I choose the next best step, even if it's a difficult one.

Clear Quartz will amplify your positive intentions and bring clarity when making decisions.

#361

I choose friendships and relationships which bring me joy, happiness and peace. Any that bring me distress I let go of with confidence and closure.

Ruby helps you move on with confidence and empowerment as you let go.

#362

I don't always know what others are going through, so
I will be kind.

Rose Quartz helps you be more considerate, patient
and loving.

#363

It's okay to be proud of yourself. It's okay to share your successes and sing them from the rooftops. At times when you are shining, pay attention to who's cheering the loudest. Surround yourself with that energy to lift you even higher.

Lapis lazuli attracts friendships on a similar level to you.

#364

I am at peace with myself. I believe in my wisdom, my intuition, and all that I am. I am amazing and I trust myself because I know that I can and will win in all areas of my life.

Carnelian raises your self-worth, inner confidence and self-belief.

#365

Let your hair down and have some fun. You've been working hard lately and it's time to reward yourself and your loved ones, and concentrate on having a good time. Dance the night away, laugh, watch your favourite film or have a meal out. Do what you love.

Orange Calcite awakens your inner joy and happiness.

#366

We urge you not to rush into making decisions that just don't feel right. The Universe has a destiny plan for you, but you should also listen to your intuition and instinct. The path ahead is full of all that you desire, good times and wonderful moments, but if you're not happy, what's it all worth? Be loyal to your cause, your feelings and align with all that you stand for. Living your truth is just as powerful as living your dreams.

Sodalite awakens your intuition and aligns your truth with your next move. This crystal will also allow you to speak with clarity and honesty, and communicate what you really need to help you succeed.

MY FAVOURITE
AFFIRMATIONS

Use this page to write down any affirmations you come
across that you wish to return to.

_____

_____

_____

_____

_____

_____

_____

_____

_____

MY FAVOURITE CRYSTALS

ETHICAL CRYSTAL SHOPS

_____

_____

_____

_____

_____

_____

_____

_____

_____

_____

ABOUT THE AUTHOR

Claire Titmus is a certified Advanced Crystal Healer and the founder of The Crystal Bar, an online store dedicated to ethically sourced crystals and mystical items. Claire uses her social media channels to share daily crystal wisdom, moon knowledge and messages of the day, alongside teaching her followers about the properties and uses of different crystals. This is her second book.

ACKNOWLEDGEMENTS

A huge thank you to Quadrille, my editor Sofie and team for helping me deliver these positive words of affirmation to the world. For having the vision to empower others to change their life and mindset for the better. What a gift we have to bestow. To my designer, Alicia, for adding magic amongst the words and adding a little sparkle amongst the pages.

To you the reader, for embracing a new path of wisdom, enlightenment and power. Without you the words would just sit on the page, but with you they come to life, they shape your future and will cheerlead you every step of the way.

Finally, to my husband Stuart and loved ones. You're simply the best. Embracing my spiritual visions, guidance and teachings. Without you my voice wouldn't be as loud, thank you for the encouragement as I travel my path of destiny.

Managing Director: Sarah Lavelle
Project Editor: Sofie Shearman
Designer: Alicia House
Cover illustrations: Vecteezy.com
Head of Production: Stephen Lang
Senior Production Controller: Sabeena Atchia

Published in 2024 by Quadrille Publishing Ltd

Quadrille
52–54 Southwark Street
London SE1 1UN
quadrille.com

Cataloguing in Publication Data:
a catalogue record for this book is
available from the British Library.

Text © Claire Titmus 2024
Design © Quadrille 2024

ISBN 978 1 83783 2101

Printed in China

FSC
www.fsc.org
MIX
Paper | Supporting
responsible forestry
FSC® C018179